Pro Choice

A Financial Guide for Women

Crystal Stranger

Pro Choice

Pro Choice

Pro Choice

DEDICATION

To my mother, Lucy. She taught me, growing up, that every day in every way we make choices that shape our lives. That if I want my life to be different, rather than complaining, I simply need to make different choices.

Pro Choice

CONTENTS

Pro Choice

ACKNOWLEDGEMENTS

Someone once said "Behind every great man, is a great woman." Well the opposite can also hold true. I am ever so grateful to my boyfriend Andre Pattantyus and all the support he has given to allow me to write books in the midst of my busy schedule of tax work and being a mom. Without him in my life, this book would likely have never materialized. I am also grateful to my daughter Synne for inspiring me to want to be a great example and make her world a better place.

Pro Choice

"MONEY IS ONLY A TOOL. IT WILL TAKE YOU WHEREVER YOU WISH, BUT IT WILL NOT REPLACE YOU AS THE DRIVER."

-AYN RAND

Pro Choice

4

INTRODUCTION

Once upon a time there was a beautiful young girl who worked so very hard, but she was picked on by her wicked family and friends. They told her she wouldn't amount to anything. Yet she kept her positive attitude up, and finally an opportunity came to make her dreams come true. Help came from unexpected avenues and she was able to attain the heights of fortune and happiness.

Does the story above sound vaguely familiar? This is the essence of Cinderella, minus the Disney princess looking for a prince to save her aspect. For a long time I disliked all these fairy tales, feeling that the message they sent was one of weakness. The helpless little princess is utterly dependent on the "knight in shining armor" to come and rescue her. But I have grown to perceive more value in this rags-to-riches tale.

We are lucky to be born in the era we are in. Until the last century, the only upward mobility a woman could have was tied to her choice of spouse. The smattering of good female examples both in ancient and recent history leaves a void of role models to choose from. Our opportunities for gaining wealth are now only limited by our ability to dream. While doing research for this book, however, I was shocked to learn how few women have taken advantage of this new world and forged lives of extreme success.

Perhaps it is because this new range of opportunity also comes with a burden. To take advantage of the birthright our grandmothers fought for, we have been granted the double edged sword of making our own choices in life. Having choices is a freedom, but also a responsibility. When we own up to our choices we've made, we gain power. We accept that where we are now is not due to circumstance, but because of choices we made. This can be a painful revelation. Yet this pain is the catharsis, taking the first step towards making good new choices by shedding the limitations of the past.

Wherever you are today, whatever you like about your life, take a moment to commend yourself for your good choices. You must first acknowledge what is working in your life before focusing on what must change.

We can have anything in life we focus on, but it is nearly impossible to have everything. There are always trade-offs and it is important to know what is already working to determine if what you want will actually enhance your life. Also, to be successful, you will need to learn when to play to your strengths and when to play to your weaknesses. Until you know what these are, it is hard to make lasting changes.

Whatever you dislike about your life, think of how you can make new choices to change those aspects. If you like your job and are generally happy in life, then you can use the information within the investment chapters to make better financial choices to save and invest your way to wealth. However, if you are reading this and find nothing of value in your life, you may wish to make a bigger change. Perhaps education, a move, or a major career change would be the choice to make, before traditional investing would come into play.

You may wonder who am I to write this book? I am a woman who was determined as a teen to learn about finance. I taught myself how to invest through reading every book in the library on investment, plus through a good dose of trial and error. I went from being homeless to millions in real estate within a few years' time, then learned accounting and created a career as an Enrolled Agent. Businesses, stocks and real estate have all been areas of investing I have succeeded within.

This book is to inspire you to make these choices, big or small, so your life can be more wonderful than you ever imagined possible. Through the choices you make now, you can be your own savior and create your life in nearly any way you can imagine. We are blessed to live in this world where we have options beyond sitting and wishing for a fairy tale ending. We are blessed to have the power to choose our own happy endings.

Pro Choice

1. PATH TO RICHES

Perhaps more than anyone else on the planet, Oprah Winfrey knows what it is like to make choices that improve one's life. She was born into extreme poverty in rural Mississippi and became pregnant at the age of 14, definitely not a start in life that would lead you to think she would become a billionaire and one of the most powerful women in the world.

The Power of Choice

There is a great power in life that comes from making choices. The one great truth is that as powerless as we may feel at moments, we always have a choice. The micro view is that in every moment we are making the choice to live by taking our next breath. On a higher level each day we choose what we do with our time, where we are, and who we spend it with. Not that every choice is available to every person all the time. Some choices are earned or eliminated by choices made in the past. Conversely the choices we make today determine what choices will be available tomorrow.

Do not dwell on the mistakes of the past either. Recognize them as mistakes you will not make again and move on. Complaining about life how it is never creates the results you want. Instead make choices to shape your future into something better.

As an investor you will make choices that determine your future. Most people don't have enough knowledge to understand how they will really come out in the end, especially after taxes, but making choices are still essential to achieving anything.

Why This Book?

This book is a progressive way of looking at investment choices with regard to finance and determining how best to make financial decisions. That is why I called this book Pro Choice.

While the knowledge in this book could be utilized by anyone, women especially have a need for financial guidance these days. I've known so many women who have more value in their handbag collection than in their retirement portfolio. While it is important to have the right clothes for career and personal reasons, it also is important to build yourself a future by saving for the long run.

Why is there such a distinct difference? Many say it is because women are more risk-adverse, so they do not take big risks that lose money. Although being described as "risk-adverse" is a bit of an underhanded compliment. It gives a glimpse into how the media truly thinks of female investors. I would claim instead that the difference is attributed to women simply viewing things differently.

> **Despite having less savings on average, women outshine men when investing:** In a report put out in 2013 by the accounting firm Rothstein Kass, it was disclosed that a sample group of 67 female hedge fund managers had an average return of 8.95% in 2012, compared to a broadly selected sample of male counterparts with a paltry return of only 2.69%.
>
> **Women are also proving more successful in business:** In 2011, a report from Catalyst found that over a five year period corporations with women on the board of directors had an average return on equity of 15.3%, while companies without any female board members averaged only 10.5%.

Defining the Difference

Women are gifted with many tools that make us inherently better at investing than men. We make up 50.8% of the population, and a far bigger share of consumer spenders, yet only hold 5.2% of Fortune 500 positions. This leaves a lot of room to out-think the old boy club, who doesn't understand intuitively how these spending decisions are made.

The basics of financial knowledge have been relatively constant for the last century. The rules of the game change at times due to legislation or cyclical trends in the market, but the essentials remain the same.

I hope this book will help you make wiser investment decisions, thereby making you wealthier. I want this because investors are the ones who build new growth and industry in our country and make this a better place. Investors are the ones who give large endowments to the arts and education. For this reason I want you to build your wealth so you can choose how to benefit our world. I trust that you will and that is the reason I'm sharing my knowledge here with you, to make our world better on so many levels.

Oprah Winfrey is a great example of someone who refused to accept her life as it seemed, and instead made new choices to create a better world. Countless others have benefited from her achievements, both as an inspiration and directly through the work she does.

Not only has she donated millions of her own wealth, she has invoked widespread change by drawing worldwide attention to many issues. In the words of Oprah, *"Understand that the right to choose your own path is a sacred privilege. Use it. Dwell in possibility."*

If I was given one wish, it would be to give you a magic wand that you can use to change your world. The fact is, you don't need a magic wand, because you already have the magical power of choice.

Pro Choice

Pro Choice

2. FOLLOW THE GOLD

Roberta Langtry was an elementary school teacher who lived a modest life in a small bungalow. Upon her death, her friends and neighbors were shocked to learn she had amassed a personal fortune in excess of 3.8 million dollars. Throughout her life she had made numerous anonymous donations of $10,000 each to individuals and families in need. It was only revealed upon her death, that she was the one who had made these donations.

How did a simple school teacher become a millionaire, and make such a difference in her community?

The Golden Rule

The key to investing is not how much you make, it is how much you keep. Anyone who has bought an investment that went through the roof, only to crash and burn, can tell you that. I read in an investment book many years ago that *"if it is not time to buy, then it is time to sell, there is no such thing as a time to hold and wait."* That advice has held true when I followed it, and unfortunately also held true when I didn't.

The golden rule is you must follow the gold. No other aspect should get in the way of this decision. When it is time to sell - sell! When it is time to buy - buy! But also keep an eye on the costs of doing business, including taxes, as this may affect how worthwhile it is to buy or sell. Taxes sometimes can even make it be a time to buy or sell, although normally that is not the case. Generally what is important, is knowing how you will stand after the deal has been completed and how much money is left over to go into the next deal.

Show Me the Money

So then, the million dollar question is: "How do I know what I will pay in taxes on this deal?" Coming from someone who has been a tax accountant for over ten years, unfortunately, the most honest answer I can give is: "There is no 100% certain way to know."

That was probably not the answer you were expecting, or wanting. It took me many years of frustration to figure this out, and this is always a concern when a client asks for forecasting. I can create general estimates of tax liability and get a good idea of how much it likely will be. Depending on the source of income it might be quite close, but there are usually aspects that will change how much tax is actually owed when tax preparation time arrives.

Taxing Investment Income

You may wonder why forecasting tax could be so difficult? When you work for wages, the taxes are withheld from your paycheck and it all balances out to rather the same amounts at the end of each year. So how could taxes be so different with investment income?

One word: Congress. Each year in either November or December, safely past election time, Congress holds meetings on budgets and presidential proposals of tax law. These rulings usually have retroactive effects and create a stir of dramatic last minute changes to IRS forms and policies.

This is rather exciting and makes being a tax accountant quite a bit more interesting than at first glance. I've never been the paper pushing accountant type, I would never last a day in an office doing bookkeeping, but I love putting together the tax and financial puzzles that come across my desk.

All the confusion, last-minute changes and grey-areas of the law - this is what makes it so fascinating. This is also what makes it a reliable career choice. Accounting was my fallback career from the acting and film production that, although it paid the bills (a major accomplishment in LA I might say), it didn't provide for much else. Eventually the glitz and glamour got old and the puzzles of finance held renewed interest.

Investing is what sparked my original interest in accounting. I had decided to teach myself stock market investing from some online tutorials and one had recommended Benjamin Graham's hefty classic, *"The Intelligent Investor"* as follow-up reading. I was completely clueless reading this book, and decided to take a college level accounting class, simply so I could understand the terminology used in financial statements better.

Reading Mr. Graham's masterpiece was rather like trying to read a book in a foreign language to me, at that time. Yet I kept trudging forward and learned a good bit about investing. Enough to transform the few thousand dollars I squirreled away into a decent down payment for my first house, within a year.

The one house grew to two, then ten, and the next thing I knew I was totally and completely at a standstill. I was paralyzed by fear of not knowing how much taxes I would owe if I sold any of my houses, them having increased in value a good bit between the market rising and renovating. I saw the top of the bubble looming, despite the surrounding buying frenzy. I wanted out but I was so scared both of losing money by selling too early if it went up, and owing money on taxes from the sales.

So many questions rained down in my mind. "Should I sell everything and use the cash to reinvest once the market has turned?" "What if I carried financing back, could I spread the tax over a few years?" "Is the gain big enough to warrant doing a 1031 exchange?" "Would I really find another property I want to buy in a 1031 exchange?" "Is it worth waiting to sell so it will be a long term capital gain?" And the questions went on and on.

I had read many books, gone to many seminars and much of the information was conflicting. Many investment advisers say to own each house in its own individual LLC. Others say to hold everything in trusts. Others say everything should be done inside a self-directed IRA. But where to even start answering these questions?

My dad has been a tax accountant my whole life, and this new interest of mine was a boon in our relationship. Finally I had something to talk about with him, but as much as he explained and we hashed out ideas, my questions about how much tax I would owe remained unanswered.

One day I was driving home from checking on workers at a property and I saw a sign up advertising the H&R Block tax course. Realizing I needed a more thorough base knowledge of taxation in general, I signed up for the course. I found I enjoyed figuring out the test clients and because of learning it for my own interests I got nearly 100% in the class.

I still wasn't closer to solving my paralyzing investment puzzle, but I finally established a solid foundation of tax knowledge. I had no interest in ever doing tax as a job and I had no need for a job at the time. The owner of the company was impressed with my proficiency and asked me to reconsider. She convinced me that as I had not answered my own questions yet, perhaps by working in the environment and having access to more research materials I would be more likely to find answers to my questions.

Seeing an element of truth in her argument I stayed on, working the whole season. After the season, I decided to pursue an Enrolled Agent training program, still trying to understand and find an answer.

Finally I found my answer: There is no

single right answer! It all depends on individual circumstances that are nuanced so tightly with the other aspects of the tax return that it is often very challenging to truly determine what is best. Take the following example:

Let's say we have a friend, we will name her Julia, who is single and makes around $40,000 a year. When you take out the roughly $10,000 of exemption and standard deduction Julia will have $30,000 in taxable income and fall into the 15% bracket, paying around $4,500 in tax.

If she sells a property and earns $5,000, that amount will fall into the 0% capital gains bracket, meaning she'll pay no tax on the additional amount and still pay a total of $4,500.

If Julia instead sells a property and earns $10,000, that will bump her up into the 25% tax bracket and she will now owe $7,500 on her wages and $1,500 on the capital gain - or $9,000 total. This is nearly double what Jane would have paid without selling the property, ouch!

It is in instances like this that tax planning is essential to investing, yet it is also is what makes it challenging. As you can see from the example, slight changes can make a world of a difference. The question then is, what could Jane do to potentially lower her tax liability? When it is already filing time, the only viable option is to contribute to a deductible IRA account. In a situation like this that is borderline on the tax rate cutoff, lowering gross income slightly can have a huge difference.

If Jane had planned in advance, she could have possibly carried a balloon payment into the next year, and split the gain between two or more years. Or she could have done a 1031 exchange and reinvested the proceeds into another property. Or she could have gifted the property to a charitable remainder trust, getting a tax deduction while not having any increase in gross income for the sale and the trust can sell and hold the proceeds until she decides to reinvest.

Maximizing Your Returns

As you can see, there are a number of choices, but you must know where you stand to make them. It is so critical in investing to be able to have the knowledge to proactively choose each step of the way to maximize benefit.

Yes, there was merit in many of the tax strategies I had questioned for usefulness, but it is important to note that if decisions are made for the purpose of tax avoidance, then generally those tax advantages will be disallowed upon examination. So decisions must be made with the strongest business purposes in mind, but with an eye to mitigating taxes owed.

Unlike many would lead you to believe, there is no single formula that guarantees wealth or success. However, one general combination has, like with Roberta Langtry, led to general success. Invest early and regularly, then maximize how much money you keep by having entrepreneurial activities and planning ahead. This is what creates long term wealth.

Pro Choice

Pro Choice

3. Deciding on Wealth

With $35 in her pocket a young girl took her first ever flight on a plane to arrive on the streets of New York, without a friend. Holding on to her dream she fearlessly self promoted her way to a record deal, then a massive media career, becoming the legendary "Queen of Pop." Today she is known as Madonna.

A friend of mine was formerly Madonna's assistant and he told me about asking her the secret of her success. Her answer was that her success was due to making decisions quickly. She would make a decision and if it didn't work out she would make a new decision. Finding success really is that simple. Most people just never make the first decision, to succeed.

Where to Start?

Amidst all the financial choices available, where do you start? First, you must learn to understand yourself and create a plan that fits your specific needs. At the end of the book I will break this down by decade and give specific tips that may help guide you for the age you are now, but these are vague guidelines.

The most important thing is to know yourself and plan accordingly. Be sure you make this a plan that gets you excited, so you have the energy and drive to carry it through.

Creating a Plan To Fit You!

First things first, where are you now? Do you have a career you are happy with? Do you own a house? Do you have someone you love and/or a close family? Are you able to travel or enjoy your hobbies? Can you help out your family and community by giving back? Do you have savings that make you feel reassured for your future? Do you want to change any of these things?

If you agree that change is needed in any of these areas, then you have a new goal. Perhaps more than one area of your life resonated as needing a change? Then you will have multiple goals to prioritize. You are the only one who can know what the most important goal for your life is, but some lead to accomplishing the others so a certain order is helpful, although not required.

Nobody gets every single thing they want in life, there are always trade-offs to be made. And you may not want to make them. If this is the case, that is fine, just choose to do that and start accepting your life is as it is now, because you are choosing to live it this way.

Building a Nest Egg

If you really are ready to change then you must be willing to make some sacrifices, at least temporarily. You don't have to live on ramen noodles and wear thrift store clothes, unless you like that, but you will have to find some areas in your life you can cut back just a little. Maybe it is making coffee at home, instead of stopping for a latte in the morning. Or packing lunches for your work week, instead of eating out all the time. These little adjustments in your schedule can make all the difference in saving.

Eating lunch out typically costs at least $10.00 these days, but you could pack a lunch from home for half that and still have a gourmet power-packed lunch.

In one year you could have put this extra $5.00 a day away in a savings account and have $1,200 to invest! That could make a significant impact to your IRA contribution, just from packing your lunch.

If you can find a way to set $25 per workday aside, maybe through cutting out Starbucks and those extra happy hour drinks, this would add up to $6,000 per year in savings!

Goals must be motivating for you, in order for them to be worthwhile. Money itself is not a very exciting motivator. But thinking about what you are going to do with that money is very exciting.

Taking the workday savings example above, you could make a decision that instead of putting the full $6,000 into savings you will put $5,000 in savings and use the extra $1,000 to take a vacation.

To motivate yourself you can use a lunchbox with your dream destination on it, or keep pictures of where you want to travel in your wallet or in your kitchen as daily reminders of why the new routine is worth it.

Perhaps central to all these goals is the very human dilemma of time vs. money. If you have the money to invest, you often don't have the time to invest it wisely, and vice versa.

Making Time to Invest

It is important to set ground rules for yourself early on as to when you see yourself fitting investing activities into your life. At least a couple hours a month is needed to look over your finances and make sure everything is in order. This is never a task one looks forward to, but necessary to obtain any lasting success. It can be fun to watch your money grow and is a good time to give yourself a little reward, like that latte you've been foregoing to save up.

Structuring Investments

Next on the decision making stratum is how do you plan using the funds you have. Financial advisers all tout the importance of diversification, but this concept is mainly given out as general strategies of percentages you should have in your portfolio. Diversification can be useful, but also can lower yields in good years and increase risk exposure during market downturns.

What is important is buying what you understand. Most of the huge stock market gains in our lifetimes have not been from clever strategies or unusual investments. They are from companies we know and use.

> Apple has gone up 8,000% in the last ten years! If you bought $1,000 of Apple stock in January of 2004 and held on you would currently have $84,513 in Apple stock.

If you rebalanced your portfolio along the way, as suggested by most investment advisers, you would most likely have far less. The likelihood is that you would have ended up losing money on some other investments you purchased, while taking money away from what was winning. I like to keep my winners working, making money for me, and sell the losing companies right away before they bring down my overall return.

Willingness to Risk

One of the reasons they say women make better investors is that we are risk-adverse. That may be true, but I don't see that as much of a compliment. Sure we won't throw away our money on foolish opportunities, but we are rarely afraid of taking new risks - or there wouldn't be so many babies born every year.

I've always seen the risk of losing out on great companies giving huge gains as more of an issue than the risk of losing money if a single company runs into trouble. But this is for gaining a nest egg. For maintaining money that has already been built up I would not be so aggressive, in that case looking for well-run companies that pay dividends is key and spreading out among sectors can help to minimize risk. I will cover this in detail in later chapters.

Strategy aside, the main thing is to commit to making choices for yourself. Then believe in your decisions. Sure some of them will be wrong, but then, just like Madonna, you will make new choices and eventually find success.

Pro Choice

Pro Choice

4. GETTING STARTED

After dropping out of high school, Sophia Amoruso bounced around from one job to another, then started selling clothes she bought from thrift stores on eBay. This business has mushroomed into a hundred million dollar clothing empire. She didn't originally envision the growth her business would have, but without taking the first step, it never would have happened. In her words, "Fortune favors the bold who get shit done."

Saving Up To Start

For most people, just saving up the initial investment funds is what keeps them from getting started. Saying that you will start next month never helps. To make any progress you need to start today. Seriously, today.

> Here is how to start: Open up your wallet and count all your cash, then go into your bank account and check your balance. Add the amounts together to get a total of your cash on hand. Open a new online savings account and transfer in 10% of your total balance. It is that simple.

Sure, it may seem challenging sometimes to keep adding the funds, but if you keep that money growing, it will give you options for the future. Putting these savings in a separate account is essential, this will give you a little more of an obstacle to keep away from spending those funds.

> Now every time you get paid put 10% of your pay into that savings account. Sometimes if you get paid twice monthly, you may have more left over after paying bills from one check to the next. If it is a struggle to pay at a certain time, you can change to paying 20% of every other check in, but be sure not to cheat on that one.

Having money in the bank gives you freedom to make future choices. Once you have spent the money, you lose that ability to choose. In the words of Sophia Amoruso, *"Money looks better in the bank than on your feet."*

No Major Sacrifices

I'm not saying to give up what you enjoy, or to look sloppy, but you don't need fifty pairs of designer heels either. Making choices about what you spend your money on, so as to be able to save, gives you greater freedom in all areas of your life.

Each of those dollars you save become little

workers that tirelessly create new dollars for you. Like little "Money Minions," this money you invest keeps working day and night to recruit more minions to the cause, making you wealthy in the process.

Reducing Debt

What about debt though? If you are in debt you must get that paid down, while still investing. The snowball method works well to build momentum and get rid of debt. Here is how to do it:

Snowball Method of Reducing Debt:

1. Take out your bills and place them in order from smallest amount owed to the largest.

2. Make minimum payments on all accounts except for the smallest one. On that account pay the highest additional amount you can afford.

3. Once you pay the first bill off, add the payment on that bill to the next bill, and keep going like that until you are

debt free.

Here's an example. Let's say our friend Julia has the following debts:

- $500 medical bill ($50 payment)
- $2,500 credit card debt ($63 payment)
- $7,000 car loan ($135 payment)
- $10,000 student loan ($96 payment)

She can squeeze an extra $300 out of her monthly budget by cutting expenses.

First she applies that money towards the medical bill- paying $350 per month.

After the second month it is fully paid off and she pays the additional $350 toward the credit card debt, making a total monthly payment of $413.

Six months later that amount will be paid off and the amount is added to paying off the car loan, with payments of $546.

The car will be paid off within 17 months, and the student loan will be paid off less than a year and a half later.

In about three and a half years she has

> paid off $20,000 in debt. After this time she will have an extra $642 monthly to invest, or $7,704 annually.

This method makes a great start to a healthy retirement portfolio. The extra funds needed for starting the snowball method can be found by cutting expenses, getting a part time job, or selling stuff laying around the house on eBay. This is both a solid way to get out of debt quickly and save up an emergency fund to keep from getting into debt again.

Pro Choice

Pro Choice

5. Investing in Yourself

Despite Ursula Burns growing up in the projects in New York, her mother instilled in her a deep belief in the importance of education. She made a point about it being the way "up and out". Her determination for education led Ursula down the path to becoming the first African American woman to lead a Fortune 500 company and the 14th most powerful woman in the world.

Getting Comfortable

Before you can accumulate wealth, you must be at a place in life where you are meeting basic needs and comfortable enough. Investing in yourself to have a basic career and home life then is the first priority, although this should not outweigh all other investments. Investing in yourself includes education, career necessities such as clothing and maintaining good health.

While not traditionally considered an investment, perhaps the greatest investment you can make is education. This concept, known coldly by economists as Human Capital, is an essential part of investing on a global scale. You should treat this concept just as seriously for yourself as when examining companies to invest in.

College Education

Education, in the traditional sense, is not everything. Although it certainly can help. Degrees open doors and many companies and lines of work require them. But they are not necessary for business success, as many entrepreneurs have shown throughout the years. However, those entrepreneurs still invested in their education in other ways, even if it was not in the traditional college sense, they put the time in to learn what was needed to succeed.

Continuous Study

Beyond college, it is important to keep on learning constantly. Invest in books and courses that propel your current career, to give yourself more choices in the future. Investing in yourself isn't just about education, it also covers the basic needs for a job or career choice. I've always believed that success is something you radiate out from your health and appearance first. It is important to dress for success and form an image that suits your career choice. Not at the expense of spending all your savings on Louis Vuitton handbags, but there is a middle ground of looking and feeling great while building a successful life.

Presentation is Everything

Choices made on wardrobe perhaps shape most what our lives become. How we present ourselves to the world and the education we gain is the connecting glue that brings us into our own. If everyone around you is negative and feel stuck in their lives, it is hard to break free of that and create the life you want.

The people in your life directly affect who you are. It generally holds true that your income is the average of the five people closest to you. If you write down the five people you spend the most time with and their income, the average of their income is most likely your income. Take the following example:

Let us imagine the following is an income breakdown of your five closest friends and what they earn:

Julie $30,000

Marina $40,000

Jessie $45,000

> Amber $55,000
>
> Christine $70,000
>
> Adding all these incomes together comes to a total of $240,000.
>
> Divide that by five and, if this was your mix of friends, it would put your income at $48,000. Really brings the point home about who you spend your time with and how they are influencing you!

Why does this hold true? We discuss our life situations and financial choices with those who are closest to us. The advice these people give you makes a huge impact on your psyche.

I'm not advising to immediately ditch your friends and family, only a sociopath would do that. Instead examining the ideas those close to you hold about money and asking yourself if this is how you want to live your life, is a place to start. The truth is that over time as you shift your ideas about money and improve your own life, a gradual change of those surrounding you happens. It's a natural process, and not always a pleasant one, but something you need to understand and accept before moving to a higher level in your own life.

Investing in yourself with education and lifestyle choices is perhaps the biggest investment you can make. This is the type of investment that is not dependent on outside forces. Situations may not always turn out in your favor, but the lessons you learn can't be taken away. They become part of the fabric that makes up who you are and makes you a strong person. This creates a solid foundation of support for being an empowered investor.

Pro Choice

Pro Choice

6. CAREER CHOICES

Being a secretary at a maid service company is not a job many would see as glamorous, or as a platform for career advancement. Fresh out of college, Kristi Mailloux, saw it as a temporary situation until she went back to school. However, she agreed to stay on after the owner offered to pay her tuition. Twenty years later she was named president of Molly Maid, heading up over 450 franchises.

Career Choice

Perhaps the biggest choice you will make in your investing life is the choice of what career you have. Apart from sleeping, the most hours spent in any activity throughout your life is working. Therefore, if you are unhappy with your work, your overall life outlook will be unhappy until you change something.

Now, I'm not advocating going out and quitting your job, or even changing careers. Sometimes the only change needed is one of attitude. Often when we get caught up in the day to day struggles of life, we feel forced into things by circumstance. This attitude alone can create much dissent with a working environment. Before you make any decisions related to your job try the following exercise:

> At the beginning of the day, before walking into your office spend a minute in your car or another quiet place thinking *"I am choosing to go to work today at _____ and it will be a fun and productive day."*
>
> Then visualize your day going well and think of pleasant moments, laughing

with coworkers, the good aspects of your work. Picture a day running smoothly until the end of the day. Then walk into the office and when you step through the door think, *"I am choosing to be here today"*.

Each time anything is a struggle throughout the day think, *"I am choosing to work here and this is the consequence of that choice, what choices can I now make to resolve this?"*

After a few days of doing this exercise you may notice you have developed a new way of looking at your job. Or you may find it just is not an environment, or career choice, that is well suited to your nature. Unhappiness is often our own way of trying to motivate ourselves to do something greater in life.

Shifting Careers

If you decide your current job is not suitable, then it is time to make a change. Do not quit your job immediately, instead make a clear plan of how to move forward.

There are four basic ways to handle this situation for a smooth transition:

1. Get a second job. Working a second part time job on the evenings or weekends will allow you to save up money to have more choices about what main career you will choose.

2. Look for a new job. If your career is enjoyable but the environment you are in is not pleasant then start searching for a new company to work for.

3. Start a company. This carries more risk and responsibility. It is best to start a company in the same career you work in now, this way you are not learning everything from scratch.

4. Seek a new career. Figure out what you would really want to do and make a plan to get the education and experience needed to transition smoothly.

My mom always said when looking for a job to think about what period of time is least useful or interesting in the rest of the spectrum of your life and find a job to fill that time.

At one point in my life I decided I liked to go out in the evenings and it was good to have some time in the mornings free to run errands, so I chose a job with a shift from Noon to 8pm that worked quite well for my needs then. Also I've often had jobs that run for a short but intensive periods, or long work day schedules, so I free up more time. Working ten hour days for four days in a week, rather than eight hour days for five, frees up an extra day to work on entrepreneurial activities, learn new skills, or just to enjoy life a bit more.

Work Environment

Location of the job you have is another way to find working freedom. I've worked remotely for many stretches in my life, and it takes more discipline to get the work done, but frees up time to run errands or do other things, as needed.

Without creating both extra time and

money it is hard to ever get ahead in life. So first things first, how can you find a few hours extra every week to pursue your goals? What can get put on the back burner? Can you watch a bit less TV? Or can you switch your work schedule to put the same amount of hours in with a day less in the office? It is important to still make time for family and leisure activities, but unless you make time for career and financial development that area of your life won't advance.

It is important to count the time and money spent getting ready and commuting when you come up with the real value of your job. If you work 40 hours a week but spend two hours each day commuting to work you actually spent 50 hours total on that job. If you can rearrange to a 4 day work schedule that will save 4 hours a week of commuting time that can be used for investment and learning purposes.

The truth of how much you are currently making at work may shock you. Let's go through an exercise to find out how much you actually take home from your paycheck:

First, figure out your monthly wages after taxes. Take out your most recent paycheck. If you are paid monthly it is easy, just use your net amount, meaning the amount you actually receive as cash.

If weekly you can take the net pay and multiply by 4.3. For bi-weekly paychecks multiply by 2.1. To follow along as an example we will take a $25/hour low level professional job and break it down as follows:

Gross Pay: $1,000/week

Net Pay After Taxes: $713.91/week

Monthly: $713.91 x 4.3 = $3,069.81

Next, subtract the following costs from your net wages to come up with your actual earnings:

- Cost of Commute - mileage driven daily multiplied by federal standard mileage rate (57.5¢ for 2015)
- Work Wardrobe - depending on your job this may or may not be an issue
- Lunch and coffee break costs
- Career costs - licenses, continuing education, gifts...

Using our young professional example:

Commute Costs: 40 mi/day 57.5¢ standard mileage rate x 5 days/week x

4.3 = $494.50

Work Wardrobe: $300/mo

Lunch: $10/day x 5 days a week x 4.3 = $215

Annual Career Licensing and Professional Memberships $300/12 months = $25/month

Total Career Related Costs: $494.50 + $300 + $215 + $25 = $1034.50

Actual Earnings: $3069.81 - $1034.50 = $2035.31

The following step is to figure out the total hours spent on work activities:

- Work Hours
- Commute Time
- Time Spent Getting Ready for Work
- Career Advancement Hours (Research, Reading, Study)

For our example again:

Work Hours: 40/week x 4.3 = 172

Commute Time: 2 hours daily x 5 days a week x 4.3 = 43

Morning Work Prep: 30 mins (.5 hours) x 5 days a week x 4.3 = 10.75

Career hours: 2 hours a week reading and research x 4.3 = 8.6

> ## Total Monthly Hours Spent on Work: 234.35
>
> The final step is to take your actual earnings and divide by the total hours spent on work activities to come up with a true hourly rate.
>
> For our example:
>
> Actual Earnings Divided by Total Work Related Hours= $2035/243.35 = $8.36 actual wage!
>
> A long stretch from the $25 an hour she thought she was making at her job, and explains why it is so hard to save when out of that $8.36 remaining all living expenses such as housing and food need to be paid.

When you go through this exercise you may be surprised how little you make, or you may commend yourself for your intelligent work choices. Depending on your career choice, you may have more or less expenses and time invested outside of work. Yet all these hours count towards earning money and should be taken into consideration when deciding on career options.

Sometimes a simpler job, or working from

home, even if it pays less hourly, can mean more money when all is considered. Taking our example from the exercise, a $10 an hour restaurant job may actually bring home the same money as that $25 an hour job if the other costs like commute, food and wardrobe are eliminated, and taxes are reduced from the lower wage. If our same young professional took a job working from home at $15 an hour she would likely come out ahead relative to the time worked, even though the pay rate cut is significant.

Opportunity Costs

The other factor to weigh in to this work decision process is opportunity costs. It is important to consider career advancement each step of the way. Often there will be job options that pay less immediately, but in the long run will give greater opportunities for movement into a new work role that yields more happiness and better pay. Kristi Mailloux followed her gut and stayed with Molly Maid, seeing she had greater opportunities there than by changing careers. This decision paid off for her by allowing her to stay in a growing company on a corporate journey to the top of the house cleaning industry. This path will be different for everyone, the important thing is to look objectively at where you are now and how this will build to where you want to be.

Pro Choice

68

7. MANAGING TAXES

When she was 16, Elizabeth Warren's father had a heart attack, leading to mounting medical bills and having their car repossessed. She had to take a job as a waitress while finishing high school and was only able to attend college because of a scholarship earned from her debating skills. Becoming a law professor at Harvard, her outspoken public advocacy was the impetus behind the formation of the U.S. Consumer Financial Protection Bureau. She is also outspoken with regard to tax reform for the middle class, something long overdue.

A Taxing Life

I'll share with you a dirty little secret - we're taxed much higher in the United States than anyone tells you. From someone who has done tax returns for expats for many years and seen financials the world over, few countries are more highly taxed that we are. Especially when you add up all the different taxes that we pay: Income Tax, Social Security Tax, Medicare Tax, Unemployment Insurance and State Tax. Then, of course, we have Sales Tax, Property Tax, Gasoline tax, Alcohol tax... the list goes on and on. Most items you purchase in the US have been taxed five times before you take them home. What you have left from your paycheck to buy those overtaxed goods with, is just a portion of what you started with before taxes.

I won't get in to where that money goes, that is another great frustration. The truth is we are stuck with taxes, they are a cost of doing business. But it is still best to pay the least amount possible that is legal, right?

Tax Flexibility

The first thing to understand is how much flexibility you have with taxes. If you work a job where you are paid wages you are limited to three areas of tax maneuvering: itemized deductions, child and education credits and retirement contributions.

Itemized Deductions

I'll save you a lot of time here - unless you own a house, pay a ton of state tax, or have a sales job where you have major expenses you, most likely, will not have any benefit from itemizing deductions. Why? You are given a standard deduction amount of $6,200 if you are single, or double that if married. Most people just don't pay more than that in itemizable expenses, unless they own a house or pay tons of state tax.

Unless your itemized deductions are a good bit higher than the standard deduction, it generally is not worth itemizing. This is mainly because if you itemize taxes this year and receive a state tax refund, you will end up having to include this state tax refund as income the following year. This will increase your adjusted gross income, limiting credits and deductions the next year. Sometimes this is still worthwhile, but must be justified by a significant tax savings this year. Also, itemizing deductions increases likelihood of audit, which is a hassle and expense that exposure to should be minimized, when viable. You can see now the types of things good accountants weigh out when preparing your return, it is not as simple as many people think.

Still, for those who are able to itemize, this can be a real blessing for the tax savings it provides. The following exercise will go through expenses and how they are calculated so you can get an idea how this works. Schedule A is the form you will use for itemized deductions, if you want to pull up the form and follow along you can find it at:

http://www.irs.gov/pub/irs-pdf/f1040sa.pdf

Itemized Deductions (Schedule A)

Going through this I will use an example of a young professional "friend" who earns $50,000 per year.

Medical and Dental Expenses

For this category you will not see the first dollar of expenses until you have more expenses than the 10% Adjusted Gross Income floor. Miles driven for medical purposes also are deductible, but at a lesser amount than for business.

Our friend pays $220/mo in insurance and had a rough year where she was really sick and had ten doctor visits of $50 copays, plus a deductible of $1,500 paid for an emergency room visit, prescriptions of $250 and a dentist visit that cost $800.

- Insurance: $2,640.00
- Doctor Visits: $500
- Deductible Paid: $1,500
- Prescriptions: $250
- Dentist: $800
- Medical Miles: 300 x 23¢/mi = $69

Total Medical Expenses: $5759

AGI Floor: $50,000 x 10%(0.10) = $5,000

Medical Deduction: $5,759 - $5,000 = $759

Taxes You Paid:

This section is for state taxes as well as real estate and personal property taxes such as the vehicle licensing fee on your car.

Our friend lives in California and doesn't own a house but pays a vehicle licensing fee on her car, giving her the following:

- State Tax Paid: $2,016
- Vehicle Licensing Fee: $56

Deductible Taxes: $2,072

Investment Interest:

This is where mortgage interest comes into play as well as investment interest, such as if you have a margin account for stock investments. Generally, interest paid on credit cards and car loans are not deductible. Total amount of home mortgage interest deductible is also limited.

Our friend has yet to buy herself a house so she has no expenses for this category right now.

Gifts to Charity:

Charitable contributions are deductible, but depending on the amount deducted the record keeping demands go up. Especially non-cash contributions, like donating clothes to Goodwill or a car, require careful record keeping. Miles driven for charity also are deductible, but at a smaller rate than for business.

Our friend donates to her church regularly, she also donated a ton of clothes that she got the receipts for. She also volunteers regularly and uses her car for church purposes.

- Cash Donations: $1,200
- Non-Cash Contributions: $300
- Charitable Miles: 1200 x 14¢/mi = $168

Deductible Contributions: $1,668

Casualty and Theft Losses:

If you had a loss from a casualty and theft and did not receive insurance reimbursement you may receive a deduction for this, but it is highly limited.

Our friend did not have any casualty or theft losses.

Job Expenses and Misc. Deductions

This is the section where nearly everyone has at least a couple deductions. But the amounts here are limited by a 2% AGI floor.

Our friend drove 10 miles weekly to make a bank run for her work. She paid $200 for an educational class for licensing she keeps for her career. She also paid $300 to have her taxes prepared.

- Work Miles: 480 miles/year x 57.5¢/mi = $276
- Continuing Education: $200
- Tax Preparation: $300

Total Misc Expenses: $776

AGI Floor: $1,000

Deductible Misc. Expenses: $776 - $1,000 = -$224. As this amount is negative her deduction is zero dollars ($0).

Adding up all the deductions for our friend we come up with the following:

Total Itemized Deductions: $759 + $2072 + $1668 + $0 = $4,499

> This amount is less than the standard deduction she receives of $6,200, meaning there is no benefit for her to itemize deductions this year.

There are a couple of instances where you will need to itemize deductions, regardless of if it benefits you, such as if you are married and filing separately from your spouse and your spouse itemizes deductions. But for simplicity we will leave this just at the basics we have already covered.

Education and Child Credits

Credits are preferable to deductions in many ways. They give a bigger "bang for the buck" than deductions as they come off the bottom line. This means they directly offset the tax owed, dollar for dollar. Generally, when you hear Congress talking about a "stimulus package" of any sort, this will mean some kind of tax credit is coming. Whether the credits will be for businesses or individuals depends on the administration, as well as what goals they are trying to accomplish.

Education credits right now are rather valuable, as far as credits go. The American Opportunity Tax Credit has the advantage of being a refundable credit, meaning you can get a refund without having paid any taxes in! These credits are limited to amounts you paid for actual education costs, generally limited to just tuition, fees, books etc. This means you can't deduct your housing costs, even if paid for on-campus housing. The maximum credit is $2,500, and up to $1,000 of that is refundable.

Some of the best credits in the tax code are related to children. For each child, you may qualify for the Child Tax Credit. This gives you up to $1,000 per child as a credit and is refundable, allowing for a refund even when tax has not been withheld from your paycheck. This credit requires earned income and is phased out for high income taxpayers. But for many families it is a great help.

The Earned Income Tax Credit is another income-based tax credit that many with, and without, children qualify for. The income levels for those without children top out at very low dollar amounts. In 2014, the credit is fully eliminated at $14,590 for single taxpayers with no children. The amounts with children are a good bit higher, $46,997 for taxpayers who are married, filing joint returns, and having 3 or more children. Keep in mind that these are the phase out amounts where the credit is fully lost, the maximums are at income levels well below this.

Retirement Contributions

Retirement contributions are one of the few ways you can reduce your income after the end of the tax year. I will cover retirement contributions in depth in the next chapter, but what is important to note now is that you can contribute to an IRA account until April 15th of the year following the close of the tax year.

This is a great advantage to many taxpayers who can reduce their adjusted gross income below certain thresholds using a deductible IRA contribution in order to qualify for credits or deductions that would be otherwise lost. Also there is a credit for retirement contributions that some taxpayers can qualify for, doubling the ways to save.

Ever Changing Tax Rules

Tax laws are constantly changing, but the knowledge of how to interpret the laws and see how it may affect your individual financial situation is timeless. Many tax professionals are afraid of writing books, or giving any advice in writing, because they may be held responsible for people misconstruing their advice. Here I must add my own disclaimer: any ideas in this book should be run past your qualified tax advisor before determining if it is appropriate in your situation.

Keep in mind that tax laws are not really black and white, they are many shades of grey based on how they have been interpreted over time. Again, this is something that changes rapidly between revenue rulings and court case results.

Interpreting Tax Laws

Amidst the financial landscape that changes upon each rising tide of trendy investments one element remains the same. Knowing how to interpret the laws and investment products for how they affect your individual situation is more important than anything in and of itself.

The truth is that the laws may vary, but what remains the same is that we all should only pay the amount that is necessary in taxes and make choices with the remainder of our money. Why would we want to pay more? Are there not more worthy charities and causes we could donate our money to than supporting the government?

I don't think our government is horrible, not in relative terms with the world at large. But I do think they could spend more wisely and I doubt most of you would disagree. I for one, would like to have a choice of what my money supports and choosing where else I put that money, such as donating to charities, is a benefit of planning for taxes.

Taxes are not inherently wrong, they are a cost of doing business in most parts of the world. The services they provide are mainly of public benefit, but I also do not believe anyone should pay more than legally required to pay.

Remember that I want you to build your wealth so you may be of benefit to our world.

How much you have left over after paying taxes, is how much you have left to invest again and that will directly influence the ways in which you are able to make this world a better place.

Pro Choice

Pro Choice

8 RETIREMENT ACCOUNTS

"There once was a speedy hare who bragged about how fast he could run. Tired of hearing him boast, Slow and Steady, the tortoise, challenged him to a race..." Mary Guthrie Essame is an excellent example of the real life application of Aesop's classic saver's tale. Working as a nurse in East Sussex England, Mary was the epitome of frugal. Wearing used clothes and shoes, and having hobbies such as knitting and gardening, she

saved every penny of her modest income, building a net worth of over ten billion dollars!

Essential to Plan

Retirement saving is not fast and sexy, but it is essential to plan for this if we want to have a comfortable future. According to a 2012 study by the Society of Actuaries, less than 29% of single older women without high school degrees are prepared for retirement. This frightening statistic is likely due to the fact that women are not encouraged to save money and take care of themselves. They are told fairy tales with the knight in shining armor coming to their rescue. Yes, the gender wage gap can be partially to blame, but as nice as those excuses are, they won't put food on the table or pay the utility bills. For that it is necessary to save at least a little every year.

Slow and steady, like the tortoise, as our retirement accounts grow, we gain true freedom and equality. The old adage is to set aside 10% of your income each month for investment. This is a good amount to start with if you are young. If you start at an older age you may need to set aside 20-25% of your income if you wish to maintain your current lifestyle in retirement.

Saving money for retirement that grows tax free, and you can take it out tax free, is not as mythical as unicorns. This exists in the well-known retirement tool, the Roth IRA, or the lesser-known, Roth 401k.

These accounts are generally the first place to start if you are young and looking to save. Why? The younger you start, the more chance it has to grow. This also means the growth is more likely to face more taxes at the end than you pay now. If you have a long horizon until retirement, you generally are just starting your career and are in a low tax bracket now. This makes it more advantageous to get tax free distributions down the line, than to get a small tax advantage now from a deductible IRA or 401k.

Time on Your Side

It is hard at first glance to understand why time is such an important element in the growth of financial assets. This is because of the power of compounding interest.

Albert Einstein wrote, "Compound interest is the eighth wonder of the world. He who understands it, earns it ... he who doesn't ... pays it." This is true because compound interest can be your best friend by giving you massive investment returns, or your worst enemy, by giving you massive debt.

Compounding interest is magical in the way it grows your money. If you could take one dollar and double it every year for 20 years do you know how much money you would have at the end? $1,048,576! Over a million dollars would be the result of that.

Don't believe me still? I'll break it down step by step in the following exercise:

This shows how a dollar compounded at 100% interest rate will grow over a 20 year period...

Year 1. $2

Year 2. $4

Year 3. $8

Year 4. $16

Year 5. $32

Year 6. $64

Year 7. $128

Year 8. $256

Year 9. $512

Year 10. $1,024

Year 11. $2,048

Year 12. $4,096

Year 13. $8,192

Year 14. $16,384

Year 15. $32,768

Year 16. $65,536

Year 17. $131,072

Year 18. $262,144

Year 19. $524,288

Year 20. $1,048,576

> *At the end of 20 years that single dollar is now worth over a million dollars!*

Pretty amazing isn't it? Of course, the challenge becomes how to double your money. It may not be that hard at the beginning, but as time goes on and the amounts increase, it becomes more of a challenge to get decent returns on your investment.

Double Your Money

It is possible to double your money each year and make this a reality, but very unlikely. In addition, taxes will often take a big bite out of this investment picture.

> If we take the same compounding interest example above, but you are in a 35% tax bracket and have to pay tax on your gains each year at the end of twenty years you will have just $22,371 in your investment account.
>
> What a difference! Paying 35% in taxes cost you over a million dollars of your pie in the sky investment.

No wonder people go so crazy to avoid taxes, although that is never a good idea. Avoiding taxes is illegal and no amount of money is worth your freedom.

But wait, this chapter was supposed to be about tax free accounts, wasn't it? Guess I get to give you the million dollars back after all - as long as that money is growing in a tax free or tax deferred account. Now what are these special accounts and how do you get one? Let's cover them below, starting with the IRA flavors then going into the business accounts.

IRA Accounts

Individual Retirement Arrangements, known generally as "IRAs", are retirement accounts that have special tax treatment. This account allows you to contribute up the yearly maximum of $5,500 for 2015, as long as you are within the income limitations, and you have earned income in at least the amount of the contribution. If you own a business where you have more expenses than income, or you exclude all your earned income with the foreign earned income exclusion, you may not qualify for making a contribution to an IRA account.

Depending on where you keep your IRA account, you will have various choices for investments. Some IRA trustees only allow you to invest in a few mutual funds they offer. Others, such as the ones at online brokerages, allow you to invest in any stock market investment. You may also have a "self-directed IRA" with certain trustees where you can invest in real estate or other investments. No matter who has your account, you are not allowed to invest in collectibles, such as art, antiques or coins.

It is important to minimize the fees in your

IRA account. High fees can have a drastic effect on the amount of money in your account down the line. The average fees for mutual funds in the U.S. is 3.14%! This can greatly reduce your retirement funds.

If you invest $100,000 at age 35 and get a 7% annualized return, at age 65 you will have $324,340 in your account if you are paying 3% in fees.

But if you are paying only 1% in fees at age 65 your account will have $574,349.

That difference is nearly double the amount, for only two percentage points of fees!

Generally, the lowest fees are with online brokerage accounts, many of which only charge you for trades and don't assess any annual fees. The highest fees are generally with hedge funds or self-directed IRAs. In the right circumstances, with the best advice and luck, these accounts can pay off and be worth the fees. But this is outside of the needs of most investors, so I will not get into details on these investments in this book.

Roth IRAs

Named after senator William Roth from Delaware, who spent nearly a decade working on getting this law passed, the Roth IRA may be one of the better tax saving accounts, especially for young investors. You contribute the money with after tax money, meaning it doesn't reduce your taxes directly. But the money when you withdraw it is tax free, so if you plan to keep the funds growing for a long time, this will benefit you greatly. Also, these amounts may qualify you for a saver's credit of 10-50% of your contribution amount!

There are income limitations as to who can contribute to the Roth IRA, with the limits for single taxpayers being phased out between $116,000 and $131,000. In general, taxpayers in this bracket, or above, are not well served by contributing to a Roth IRA. More often they would benefit more from taking a deduction against their taxable income by contributing to a traditional IRA account.

An additional benefit to a Roth IRA is that that the contributions, but not earnings, can be taken out at any time without penalty. So it gives more flexibility if an emergency comes up and the funds are needed. However, if the earnings are withdrawn early, they are subject both to income tax and the 10% additional penalty tax, so it is not wise to fully cash out a Roth IRA.

Traditional IRA

In general, if you are in a 25% tax bracket or above I would recommend using a traditional IRA rather than a Roth IRA. This is contrary to what many advisers say, but I think the logic is rather obvious - 25% more money now from tax savings can be worth paying tax down the line. Let's look at a comparison:

Our friend Jane is 45 years old and contributes $5,500 into a Roth IRA.

She makes around $100,000 a year, is in a 28% tax bracket, and as this is an after tax contribution, she receives no tax deduction.

After ten years at 6% compounded interest her Roth IRA has grown to $9,849.

After twenty years it is $17,639 and she can withdraw from this tax free.

Shelly also is 45 years old, makes the same income as Jane, but contributes her $5,500 into a deductible traditional IRA.

She invests her additional tax refund of $1,540 in a tax-free municipal bond.

Her traditional IRA has also grown to $17,639. She rolls it over into a Roth IRA so it won't be taxed in the future, but she is retired and in a lower tax bracket now and will only pay 15% tax, leaving her with $14,993 in her Roth IRA.

The additional amount invested in the muni bond at 5% interest has grown to $4,086.

> **Added together this leaves her with a total of $19,079 of tax free savings- $1,440 more than Jane!**

This 8% of additional savings is just a small example, but can have a bigger effect with larger amounts of investments, and higher tax brackets. The shorter the time period to invest, the bigger the difference will be seen in your overall portfolio assets.

In general, if your timeline for investing is less than 25 years and you are in a current tax bracket of 25% or more, it will be more advantageous to take the tax deferral from a traditional IRA or 401k rather than paying after-tax money into a Roth IRA.

One downside of a traditional IRA is at age 70½ there are mandatory distribution amounts that must be taken, otherwise a penalty tax is imposed. With the distributions being taxable this can push one into a higher tax bracket and make social security taxable. Also, if funds are withdrawn before retirement age there is a 10% penalty tax in addition to the increase in taxable income. That is why cashing out a traditional

IRA or 401k should only be an absolute last resort.

401k Plans

If you are offered a 401k at your job, especially one with a matching contribution, it is to your benefit to maximize your contribution. With employer matching, this is like getting a free raise. The other great benefit of contributing to a 401k is the monies you invest are taken out before you see them, making it easy to save.

Now many 401k's come in both traditional and Roth flavors. Which type is most beneficial to contribute to depends on your tax bracket and timeline to retirement. If you are in a tax bracket of over 25% and have less than 25 years until retirement age, it is beneficial to max out your traditional 401k contributions and lower your current income tax. If you have a longer investment timeline you may be better off maximizing your investment dollars in an after tax Roth IRA or Roth 401k, if that is available to you.

As with traditional IRAs, 401k plans require

distributions at age 70½, and distributions are taxable when received. Many 401k plans have vesting requirements, where you have to stay with a company for a certain amount of time before the funds are available. Also you generally cannot have access to the funds until quitting the job. This means, in some cases, quitting your job to have access to the funds to reinvest more wisely can be a smart decision.

SEP IRA

The Simplified Employee Pension Plan, or SEP IRA, is a plan created for small business owners, even those with no employees. Using this plan, self-employed investors can take part in retirement savings that they are missing out on from not working in a larger company.

With a SEP plan only the employer contributes, so this can be a good plan if cash flow is an issue. However, contribution amounts must be equal for all employees, so this can become expensive for companies with many employees and is why these plans are typically used just for very small businesses.

Defined Contribution Plan

If you own your own business it may be worthwhile to set up your own retirement plan for yourself and your employees. One way to do this is with a Defined Contribution Plan.

Essentially this is a 401k, but as it is set up a bit differently the limits for contribution amounts are higher. Contribution amounts can be up to 25% of wages, and must be mandatory. Up to $53,000 can be contributed for 2015 to a Defined Contribution Plan spread between employer and employee contributions.

When you set up a Defined Contribution Plan, you must also offer this plan to employees, so usually this is done in small companies as the profit share portions are large. Sometimes these plans are offered just to key employees. As the rules for these plans are quite complex, if you are able to benefit from setting more tax free money aside from your business like this it is advisable to get professional help in establishing and maintaining this plan.

Defined contribution plans can carry high expenses for opening and maintaining the plan.

These expenses must also be figured in to the value before deciding this is the most beneficial way to go and whether this will provide sufficient savings to warrant the cost and effort.

Defined Benefit Plans

These plans are becoming far less common in the US now, villainized as the pension plans that sunk whole industries in their antiquated ways, but Defined Benefit Plans can be a valuable investment, especially for successful small business owners. These plans essentially purchase an annuity stream of income that provides equal payments for the remainder of an employee's life after retirement, or are self-administered to do the same thing.

Like other annuity streams, this can be a good for those nearing retirement age, and having the benefit of making payments with pre-tax money if you pay for this out of your company, can be a double savings. Through these plans, around $100,000 a year can be set aside before taxes, making them a great option for high earning entrepreneurs.

The Big Picture

The type of retirement account you use is less important in the long run than that you start saving for retirement now. Part of the beauty of these accounts is that it makes it harder to tap into these funds, giving discipline to saving.

Not to crush your dreams of retiring as a billionaire like Mary Guthrie Essame, but without saving now you won't have a comfortable retirement at all. You may like enjoying the jet set lifestyle now, but it that worth living off cat food for your golden years? Slow and steady sink at least small bits of money away now to provide for a comfortable future, you will thank yourself down the road.

Pro Choice

Pro Choice

9. Cash Accounts

Patsy Cline grew up on the wrong side of the tracks. After her father left she dropped out of high school to work part time jobs and support her family. Her success was tied to providing for her family and she understood the importance of cash. In her words, *"Boys, they can't take my refrigerator now. They'll never get my car now. I paid cash for 'em and they're mine, and I'm keepin' 'em!"*

Emergency Funds

Having cash, as well as a healthy emergency fund, is critical to achieving any sort of financial success. In Chapter 3 we discussed the snowball method of getting out of debt. Conversely, having cash on hand is the secret to stay away from the snowball method of getting into debt.

My family was really into saving money. When my mom and I cleaned out my grandmother's house after she died, we found one linen closet with nearly $5,000 stashed away in various places - no single stash over $100. They taught me it is important to always have emergency money on hand, and to never spend money before having it. This is an example I try to live out for my daughter as well.

But how much emergency money should one keep on hand? A good place to start is three months' worth of pay. Within a year of saving you should be able to put this amount aside, and it will cover most small disruptions to life such as having car trouble or a minor health issue. If you are thinking of making a major career change, it is wise to save up a full year's worth of wages. This can be accomplished by getting a second job for a time, or maybe you have some items around the house you could sell in order to increase your savings?

If you own your own business, you should be doing cashflow forecasting and keeping a minimum of six months liquid capital in an easily accessible business account. This will prevent the "liquidity squeezes" that lead to businesses taking on harmful types of debt, like high interest credit cards or short term credit lines from the loan sharks of the business world.

Holding Investment Funds as Cash

Many investment advisers recommend keeping a portion of your investment funds in cash. But, aside from the emergency funds I mentioned before, I don't think that is a good idea. Keeping a portion of the investment funds as cash is foolish, those dollars are not working to give you a return, so they are just sitting there. Lazy dollars don't lead to high returns.

What then to do with cash accounts? This money must be kept somewhere, and stuffed inside a closet is not the safest place for storing funds. An interest earning bank account is the obvious next best choice. Money market accounts, or even short term CDs, can also be good, as can a Treasury.gov account.

Banking Relationships

My grandfather had bank accounts at twenty different banks. He would go to a different bank each day during the week to put a small deposit in, while having a free cup of coffee and cookies. He always took the time to chat with the bank managers and everyone knew him. He stressed to me the importance of having good banking relationships.

Having a banker know you means there is someone you can walk in and see if you have a problem with your account and they will help you. Yes, they should do this with everyone, but banks are preferential to the people who keep more money in them.

There are often advantages to keeping minimum sums in your local account. Generally, in the $5,000-$10,000 range, banks offer premium accounts that give you benefits such as free check printing and a safety deposit box. The value of these services can range from $50-$100 per year, and are often more of value than the additional interest that a higher paying account would give.

These days, with all the online options, there are less personal relationships with banking and finance. But it still comes in handy if you can build a relationship with your local banker. This doesn't work well with the big banks, in general, although they can have other benefits.

> I would recommend having accounts with two banks for two separate reasons:
>
> 1. A local account that you use most often and if there are any problems you have someone you can work with on solving them. Also it is a good idea to have a safety deposit box for your important paperwork.
> 2. An online bank account to get a higher rate savings and freedom of accessibility while travelling or if you move.

Hidden Fees

It is important to also keep an eye on the hidden fees. Monthly charges for things like

ATM usage, or overdraft charges can really add up. Most people don't know that an overdraft is an optional service and you can deny this and avoid all the fees that may result. This means your card gets declined if you try to use it and there isn't money in the account, but isn't that better than paying $34 per item for each charge?

For investment accounts, I would skip the local brokers and managed accounts to go directly with an online brokerage. This gives you full control of your investment choices rather than just a few funds to choose between.

Structuring Cash Holdings

Perhaps not as important as having cash saved up, where you keep it can also be important. The following is an example of how bank accounts can be structured:

> *Our friend, Ida, has been saving for the last couple years. She has accumulated $6,000 as an emergency fund and $5,000 for investing. As income she has $2,000 a month come*

in from her job and $600 a month from her Etsy page where she sells knitted hats. This is one good possibility of how she could structure her banking life:

Local Bank Accounts: Checking account plus a connected savings account with the $6,000. At most banks by keeping this amount of a balance, she should qualify for some level of premier banking services that will give her free checks, wires, and other bank services. Usually the value of these services will be worth $50-100 per year, far more interest than the $6,000 would earn in a higher interest paying online account.

Online Accounts: Have a separate online personal checking and savings account used for her Etsy business. This way she can save her profits separately from the business activities, giving her a nest egg to expand the business from, when she is ready. Also keeping the income and expenses from this activity separate allows her to make her tax filing easy at the end of the year.

Investment Account: Ida sounds like she is in a good position to have a discount brokerage where she can manage how she invests her funds directly. Since she doesn't want to choose individual stocks she goes for a company where she can invest in sectors, and chooses to place $1,000 in five different sector index funds.

Wherever you end up holding your funds it is important to remember these funds are for emergencies only, and that vacation to Tahiti or big sale at Macy's doesn't count as an emergency. Remember to also keep the credit card usage to a minimum, having something now is rarely as long lasting of a good feeling as the confidence that comes from knowing you have money in the bank.

Pro Choice

Pro Choice

10. INVESTMENT CHOICES

As a college dropout in the 1950's, Muriel Siebert started out doing research for Wall Street institutions. Frustrated with the wage and career disparities she founded her own firm Muriel Siebert & Co. and became the first woman to own a seat on the New York Stock Exchange. She also turned her firm into one of the first discount brokerages in the mid 70's, paving the way for everyone to be able to make their own investment choices.

What to Invest In?

Now that you have started your investment accounts, what do you invest in? The most important thing is to understand what you invest in.

Many unscrupulous investment advisers play into the fear and greed of their clients, and sell them complex investments that few understand. These occasionally are wildly profitable, but more times than not they are simply a way of separating the client from their hard earned money. In general, the more complex an investment is, the more easily someone can be siphoning money out of it without investors figuring it out.

There are three basic elements to making a wise investment:

1. Choosing the company or industry that will be the winner for you. (this chapter)

116

2. Timing your purchase by understanding the market and industry. (Chapter 11)

3. Understanding the finances of a company so you can know if it is in good shape. (Chapter 12)

Ownership is Key

The golden rule is to think of yourself as an owner in anything you invest in. No matter how small your investment, if you buy a stock you are an owner of the company you are buying. You should also understand the business and believe in what it does. If you are a doctor, you are in a good position to buy pharmaceutical companies. If you are a mechanic, then auto suppliers and gas companies are good choices. If you have kids then you will be well versed in consumer goods companies. All of these areas will have undervalued companies that you have the knowledge to see the value in, you just have to look for them.

Similarly, if you are buying bonds you are loaning money to a company or municipality, so you should know the company as well as for a stock purchase, or follow the politics of that city and what the funds are being used for. With real estate, you should buy properties that you feel comfortable owning, preferably ones you can drive by easily to check on.

Shop Away!

Shopping is great fun. Whether shopping for shoes, purses, stocks, or real estate, women are naturally gifted at finding the best values for our money. We all love the hunt and this is just a new game to make use of those same skills we've spent a lifetime developing. Actually there is a direct crossover. The same companies you search for in stores and online for clothes and household goods can be great investment picks. It is investing power to know the hot brands and see which stores are packed with people and which ones are turning into funeral homes long before that information hits Wall Street. The buyers who shop and make the choices in the store are the ones in the long run who determine which companies succeed.

When I was a little girl my grandfather used to take me shopping during our visits each fall, and he paid close attention to what toys and brands I was interested in. Turns out he was buying and selling stocks based on what my interests were and he started giving me money each year when I visited, to thank me for the good stock tips I gave him!

These are the sources of financial information you should look for, rather than tips on TV or in a magazine. When you walk through the stores, notice which brands sell out and then look them up online and find out who the the parent companies are. Don't just buy right away, examine in depth if they should be a good investment. How to do exactly that we will cover in chapter 9, understanding financial reports. But let us first understand all the general ideas of what can be invested in.

Children are especially great investment guides, they are usually on the pulse of everything cool. What they wear, play with and eat are the crux of what the American public is buying. Why is this true? Who wants to deny their children any enjoyment? We have a culture based around the importance of our next generation. I understand this personally, my daughter is the center of my world and I hope to teach her many good ideas about finance as she grows up, including the concept of delay of gratification, but I still give in and spoil her now and then.

Sorting the Choices

How do you know when the hot toy of the season will be a company that is a good buy? The first part is to find out how big the company is and how many other toys they have as this will determine if the stock will be affected by this new offering.

> If Mattel makes a hot toy, their stock won't gain from it as much as if the toy is made by a small company where it is the main item driving the sales figures. Mattel needs to have big hits each year just to stay in business.

Large companies like this can be a good buy at times when the price has dropped on market fears or at any time if they have strong management, for long term holds in your portfolio. Dividend payouts are key to watch in that case.

Good management means more than almost anything else. Just watch any of the movies or documentaries about Steve Jobs if you have any doubt whatsoever about the power of investing in companies with visionary management. Not all companies will have this and it is often easier to see this in retrospect, but management can be one good determining factor to buy or sell.

Next you must understand the products or services the company you are interested in sells. I will continue to use the toy example for simplicity:

Are all the toys they sell brands you are familiar with or have they just marketed a few while having other items taking up inventory space, but not selling?

Are the toys not durable enough? If they break too easily parents won't re-buy them and the company may be at risk of lawsuits from injuries.

> Are they too durable? If they last forever, who will buy them down the line?
>
> Are they coming out with improvements on the toys that make children want more? Think of Barbie as an example, if they only made one basic Barbie forever it wouldn't have been as lasting as all the trendy and seasonal variations that are released.

Whatever you invest in, remember that the markets are ruled by fear and greed. Opportunities abound in doing things differently than what everyone else is doing. There is power in thinking for yourself. As Muriel Siebert once said: *"The real risk lies in continuing to do things the way they've always been done."*

Pro Choice

Pro Choice

11. TIME ON YOUR SIDE

One day, Sara Blakely cut the feet off a pair of pantyhose to wear under white pants, so they would look more trim. This idea led to her launching Spanx two years later. Once she launched her product, she put every effort into selling it, forming retail partnerships and gaining many celebrity endorsements. Her intense launch of her product allowed it to find the right market, rocketing her to the heights of success. By 2012, she was the world's youngest self-made female billionaire.

Timing is Everything

Women always know that timing is everything in life. They often have an innate knack for this, giving them an advantage in both business and investing. We have all seen trends come and go. Women learn at a young age when it is time to ditch those leopard print pants for the next style. Just like clothing, some products or investments have seasonal ebbs and flows and are affected by market trends.

Trying too hard to time the market can drive one insane, so I don't recommend that by any means. However, it is important to understand the cyclical nature of the markets and especially certain types of investments. Knowing when to buy and when to sell is how you achieve more than mediocre returns.

Technical Investing

One major branch of traditional investment is based on timing the markets, based on viewing charts and other indicators. Known as "Technical Investing" there are many books and tools out there to follow these trends, although they only show one side of the picture - the general trend of how the public is reacting to a stock. There are many books and articles on this subject if you would like to use more, but the bottom line is there will always be those with better computer models and tools viewing these trends. That is why speculating purely on technical trends is incredibly risky. These activities are best left to hedge funds who have the computer models and technicians ready with their finger on the button, poised to invest before others.

Still, without understanding how Wall Street views a company you are interested in, you risk losing money even on good companies. Generally there are two cycles that people vacillate through about companies: fear and greed. Many say to buy when the market is fearful and sell when the market is greedy, but it is not as simple as that.

Double the Gain

If you buy into a company when the price is going down, every drop takes twice the gain to come back. Many fortunes have been lost from not truly understanding this risk.

If a stock drops 50% in value it takes a 100% gain to come back to where it started.

For example, our friend Gerri bought 100 shares of XYZ stock at $10 a share. It drops to $5, leaving her with $500, or a 50% loss.

Our friend Renee sees XYZ as a turnaround and buys 200 shares at $5 a share thinking the price will go up. It goes back up to $10 a share, making her $1,000, or a 100% return!

Gerri then decides the stock is destined to go down again at $10 and decides to make a short sale of 100 shares. But instead of going down the stock then shoots up to $30 a share, Gerri then has lost $2,000 - double what the initial investment of $1,000 at $10 a share would have been, or a 200% loss!

This is why shorting stock, thereby betting on it going down, is such a risky move. Shorting a stock, the maximum you can earn is the descent to zero, but the potential to lose money is unlimited! Also, in the long run inflation will push the market up, meaning betting on it going down will only work for so long.

Rising Markets

In general, the market always goes up. But I'm not a huge fan of "buy, hold and pray" either. Different strategies are needed at different times. Having a general understanding of both the economy and investment types will give you some knowledge towards making educated decisions.

Every investment runs on a slightly different timeline, although it is not as divided as the diversification devotees would have you believe. If there is a big enough downturn, it hurts most investments.

Stock, bond, and real estate markets have all triggered each other having drops. These dips can be very localized, or universal, but there is no real safety in following the diversify, hold and pray methodology. Not that diversification isn't important, I still believe in it, but not for safety from downturns but rather from the direction of keeping options open to find the most successful companies.

Downturn Investments

Some investments do better in down-times. Traditionally low cost items or necessities, like grocery stores and fast food chains are good for storing value during tough times. General human needs such as food and shelter are universal. Good times or bad, people will spend to survive. Discount chains such as Wal-Mart or dollar stores, tend to have big gains amidst slow markets.

Other investments, such as tech companies and business to business services tend to do best with a growing economy. This is because as the economy grows, businesses spend their extra funds to keep up with growth and to stay ahead of their competitors.

Dependent Investments

Many investments are driven by external factors, such as oil or other commodity prices. Right now, the price of oil has dropped by 50%, this will be a huge stimulus to many firms in the coming months as their transportation, heating and manufacturing costs decrease. But other companies who build equipment for oil drillers or are involved in oil production in any way, will suffer.

Cyclical Investments

Some investments, such as automobiles, are cyclical. This means they run on their own cycles that have little correlation with the overall market. Think about it this way: If you bought a brand new car five years ago and it still runs perfectly, you may want to trade in your car, or you may wait a bit longer depending on your finances. Also, car companies are forced to make major changes every handful of years and all the investment in new tooling is expensive and can be difficult for them to fund. If a company takes on too much financing for these purposes just before a recession hits, the financials of the company can be stressed to the the point of bankruptcy. We saw this happen to several of the major US car companies in the last downturn.

Market Sentiment

The overall optimism of the market has a huge influence as well. If people feel hopeful for the future, they invest their savings in the stock market. If they are fearful, they will pull funds out and wait for a better day. The trouble is, by the time most people reach the state of fear or optimism where they take action, it is late in the game and they have lost most of the gains. Or worse yet, lost half their savings.

How then to know when to buy or sell? Buying is fairly easy. Do the research and you will understand clearly if the company is on the way up, or on the way out. Selling is more challenging though. The only real answer I've found in years of investing is that if it's not time to buy, it's time to sell.

It is important to take a look at each of the investments you own once a month and ask yourself the question, "Would it be a good idea to invest more money in this company now?" If the answer is not a resounding "yes" you then must look at if it is time to sell. Remember of course, that just because it would be profitable to invest more in a company does not mean that is your best bet, just that it isn't time to sell yet.

Rather, you may find a better investment somewhere else to put new money in. Some companies have such good management that there is never a time to sell. Their long term stock prices are evidence of this.

This rule of "selling if it is not time to buy" reaches beyond stocks. When I was a real estate investor, I found as the market got near the top it was harder and harder for me to find bargains. When very few bargains were available and houses needing everything done were nearly as pricey as ones that were fixed up, I should have taken it as a time to sell. This can be hard to see though, our own greed often clouds our vision. It is always better to sell a bit too early and miss out on some of the profit, than to lose money on the way down, or not to be able to sell at all.

Timing in life is important beyond investing and into the business world. Timing is important not just for when you push your product to the world, but also for when you hold back and wait. Introducing your idea before the market is ready can be an exercise in frustration, or negative feedback can stop a good idea before it has a chance to find a market.

Sara Blakely kept her undergarment idea under wraps for the first year while developing her prototype. Only when she was ready to launch did she share her idea with family and friends. In her words, *"Don't solicit feedback on your product, idea or your business just for validation purposes. You want to tell the people who can help move your idea forward, but if you're just looking to your friend, co-worker, husband or wife for validation, be careful. It can stop a lot of multimillion-dollar ideas in their tracks in the beginning."*

Pro Choice

135

Pro Choice

12. THE NUMBERS LIE

At the age of 40, Geraldine Weiss had been rejected by every Wall Street firm she applied for a job at, offered only secretarial positions despite her education and history of investing. She founded a newsletter under the name G. Weiss in 1966 and only revealed her true identity ten years later on a talk show after nobody cared she was a woman, because she had made them so much money. Her newsletter beat the market every year except one, giving an annualized return of 19.1% during its existence.

This rivals Warren Buffett's 19.8% annualized return, making this all but unknown woman the second best investor in history! How did she achieve such investment success? By using a value investment formula tracking dividend yields to determine the truth behind corporate finances.

Finding the Truth

Corporations sometimes seem like strippers, dressed up to the nines plastered in makeup, selling a dream. We've all seen what the right clothes and makeup can do, corporations do the same things with their glossy annual statements and glowing press releases. But the truth lies in the numbers, like weight on the scale, they do not lie.

Financial reports are complex. There are many areas within them that can be adjusted by clever accountants to paint any picture they like. In the words of Geraldine Weiss:

"Earnings are often subject to those vague bookkeeping practices such as depreciation, cash flow, inventory adjustments and reserves. A skillful accountant can make good earnings appear not-so-good, and vice-versa, depending on tax considerations. Or the motive for

manipulating earnings may be much more sinister than the minimization of tax liability. A company may want to puff up its quarterly earnings to enhance the share price of a pending stock offering. Certain companies have even been accused of depressing earnings in one quarter to allow officers and directors to earn their stock options at a lower price and sell them at a higher price when subsequent delayed earnings are heftier."

Picking Winners

So how did Geraldine Weiss break these numbers down to pick her winners? She determined the one element that accountants can't manipulate is how much dividends are paid out. That is real cash sent out to shareholders each year. A company with a history of paying consistently increasing dividends shows good management. Below is the criteria she would use to pick stocks, beautiful in both its simplicity and thoroughness.

GERALDINE WEISS STOCK SCREEN

Objective

To uncover high-quality blue-chip stocks quoting at near their historically high dividend yields.

Primary Criteria

Criteria to locate stocks that match our screening objective

1. Dividend increases in 5 of the last 12 years – Weiss's most reliable measure of good management.

2. Improved earnings in at least 7 of the last 12 years.

3. Must have paid dividends with no interruptions.

4. Current dividend yield within 10% of the company's historically high dividend yield.

Secondary Criteria

Criteria to ensure companies passing the primary screen do not meet the objectives just by coincidence, but

> *because they are deserving candidates. Useful to eliminate poor performers from creeping in.*
>
> 1. A minimum of 5 million shares outstanding - An assurance of liquidity.
>
> 2. Shares must be held by at least 80 institutions.
>
> 3. Stock must carry a S&P quality ranking of at least A- or above.

This is one of the most comprehensive ways to pick stocks I have ever come across, at least from the financial perspective. There are many other theories on how best to buy stocks, ranging from asset plays to technical investing that buys on market trends. It is hard to play many of these games though, as unless you devote yourself full-time to this endeavor there will always be investors more sophisticated who will win at your expense.

Early Growth

Weiss' system leaves out many early growth

companies that may have spectacular gains. For these companies, it can be hard to gauge based on the financials alone, sometimes great management and opportunity warrants purchasing a company with less history. But losing money is no fun either. Be sure if you are going to buy riskier companies that what you find with the Weiss formula that you watch your stocks every month and sell if you start to lose money. Never risk more than you can afford to lose.

> Generally, if a stock I buy drops 7%, or one I've owned for a while goes down 15%, I will sell it. I may repurchase it at a later time, but I like to limit how much I can lose. This can be programmed in to online investment accounts so as to be automated, saving me from needing to watch stock prices all day to make determinations of holding or selling.

When using online investment accounts you can typically set "stop loss" orders to minimize losses on new purchases should the price drop below a certain point. I usually add this when I purchase a new stock as insurance for timing this and update my existing stocks monthly. I don't want to lose too much if I buy in at the wrong time.

Learning to Understand Financials

The main reason learning about financials is so important, is to give you confidence in your choices. This way if some broker grills you on a company having a substandard P/E or growth ratio, you will know enough to tell if they are talking out their you-know-whats.

For thoroughly learning how to understand financial statements, I would suggest reading more investing books and following the TV shows that discuss this. Peter Lynch's books are especially easy to read and Mad Money is entertaining in the way Jim Cramer cuts through all the market B.S.

I especially like when the financial shows air interviews with CEOs. This gives me a good bit of insight into a company by how the top dog will avoid certain questions. Another great female skill is usually telling who is lying, which is a big advantage when dealing with corporate

America. I always enjoy watching them talk, wondering what secrets they are hiding.

Pro Choice

Pro Choice

13. STARTING A BUSINESS

When Diane Von Furstenberg became engaged to a German prince, she decided the life of being only the wife of someone famous was not for her. She founded her eponymous clothing line and built a multi-million dollar fortune, motivated by this belief. In her words, *"I wanted to be someone of my own, and not just a plain little girl who got married beyond her desserts."*

Long Way to the Top

To have real freedom and recognition in the world, creating your own business can be the way to the top. It is not, however, easy money by any means. Starting and running a business is not for everyone, but for those who can cut it, there is much freedom and financial reward available.

It can be terrifying to venture out into the uncertain waters of business ownership. Depending how you face that fear, is a big element of whether or not you are successful. Diane Von Furstenberg's mother was a Holocaust survivor who taught her that "Fear is not an option." To be successful in business, that is the type of motto that must be adopted.

Not the Easy Road

Starting a business is the clearest way to the top. Few have become wealthy without owning their own business. But for just being comfortable and financially secure there are easier ways to go. The key is you have to have real passion for the business you build. If you aren't doing what you love, you might as well be doing it for someone else. Then when you get sick of it you can walk away.

When you own your own business the responsibilities are bigger. You will have employees and bills to pay that can make it seem a lot less freeing than at first glance. But the rewards, both personal and financial, can far outweigh the drawbacks.

Deciding on an Enterprise

What kind of business should you start? Something you know well. Start with what you already do for a living or a hobby and build a money machine around that knowledge. Don't go out and try something totally new, just learning to be in business is hard enough without learning the skills you need as well.

Whatever you are doing for work now, there are probably opportunities to offer your services as a business instead of working for wages.

If you have not signed a non-competition

agreement with your company, you can go right in to starting a side business in the same line of work. Just be sure not to cross that ethical boundary of stealing clients from your boss, as that rarely ends well.

If you can't do the same line of business immediately, then maybe you can go into business doing something else you love.

If you love animals you could start a dog-walking or pet sitting business.

If you have good organizational skills you could offer help to others.

You can even turn destructive habits into money. If you spend too much time on social media you can offer this as a skill to businesses that need help with networking.

Your mind is your only limit - start thinking what you can provide to the world. The more people you help, the richer you will become!

The important thing is to get out there and try what you feel drawn to do. Those intuitive urges are there for a reason, we should make use of them as best we can. The first thing you try often will not be the business you find success with. Unless you get out there and try, you will never build the skills needed to someday succeed at the business that will really pay off.

Social Entrepreneurship

Social entrepreneurship is especially becoming popular these days. Is there a business you could start that will both improve the world around you and give you financial stability? In general, businesses become successful because they fill a need. The more people you are able to help with your business the more successful you will come, both financially and spiritually.

Follow Your Passion

Passion is critical in business. If you are not passionate about what you are doing, then you will not have the lasting power to hold on through the testing times. There will always be testing times, when it does not feel like anything will ever work out.

These testing times are one reason it is best to start businesses part time, while keeping your day job. This gives both the financial stability to wait out the tough times and the motivation to make the business a success so you can quit the other job.

Martin Luther King said, *"Faith is taking the first step even when you don't see the whole staircase."* Starting a business is the time in life when your faith will be most tested. But hang in there, persevere, and you will be rewarded with riches and freedom beyond your imagination.

Pro Choice

Pro Choice

14. Real Estate

Starting with a $1000 loan, Barbara Corcoran used her common sense ideas to build a billion dollar real estate empire. Now she is an investor on the ABC show, "Shark Tank" and has helped many entrepreneurs by investing in their ideas and guiding them to success. Her inspiring real estate investing motto is, *"Taking chances almost always makes for happy endings."*

Real-Life Monopoly

Did you like playing Monopoly as a child? Real estate investment in real life is essentially the same. Buy whatever you can afford at the beginning, try to get properties concentrated together, buy several little houses and rent them out for more and more money, then trade up for bigger properties. Yes, it really is that simple. It also can feel just as slow, boring and frustrating as the game at times, but is great when successful.

Real estate is something everyone uses. Everyone needs a place to live, right? Historically it has held some of the highest investment returns, but can carry more risk than many investors realize. I've done very well in real estate and I think most women are capable of making a fortune this way, but I won't lie, it is hard work.

Should You Buy Your Own Home?

Buying the house you live in is one of the choices that I feel people are least well advised about. If you go to a real estate agent and ask if you can buy a home they will figure out the maximum mortgage you can qualify for, then show you houses at that level. For most people, this greatly increases your monthly cost of living, leaving less left over for investing.

Your home can be a good investment, and tax-wise it is one of the best, but it has to make sense from a monthly cash flow perspective. Below are some examples of when and when not to make the jump from renting to buying.

If you are paying $1,500 a month in rent and it will cost you $3,000 a month in total payment to buy, that is not a good decision. If you can afford this, great!

Set the extra $1,500 a month aside to invest or buy a rental or vacation property somewhere else to have some equity while renting the house you live in.

That extra savings can buy a nice second home, and you can probably rent that out at least part of the year if you buy in the right location. Without it needing to be near your job, you have much more choices than buying your residence, and you will still be gaining equity in rising real estate markets.

If you are paying $1,500 a month in rent and it will cost you $1,000 a month to buy, what are you waiting for??? Buy immediately, buy more than one place and rent the other one out, just buy something now.

If you are paying $1,500 a month in rent and it will cost you $2,000 a month to buy you will have to make a hard decision. The extra cost is negligible at this rate with the trade-off of gaining equity by paying down a mortgage.

If prices are within reason and you are planning to stay in the same neighborhood for at least the next few years, you will usually benefit from buying. The cost of rents always go up with time, but the cost of a mortgage is locked in for the timeline you set when buying. When rents and purchase prices of houses are not too out of line, buying will always be of benefit in the long run, and gives a certain pride of ownership that makes one feel like a good investor.

Timing the Market

What then about timing the real estate market? Real estate runs in very long cycles and it can be tough to judge when real estate values will go up. Thus carefully choosing the individual properties you can build value in from creatively seeing what the property can be, is a safer choice then just waiting for the market.

The first apartment Barbara Corcoran rented out she had the vision to add a wall to make it a one bedroom with a den. By doing this she was able to immediately rent it for an extra $20 a month, endearing her to the manager.

As another example, I bought a property once that had three additional lots that were combined just for property tax purposes. I split the property into separate parcels and six months later sold the three lots for ten times what I had paid for the house, then owning the house free and clear.

The important thing is to get in the market now so you can benefit from the long term gains, assuming it makes sense for you from a financial perspective. In the words of Barbara Corcoran, *"A funny thing happens in real estate. When it comes back, it comes back up like gangbusters."*

Pro Choice

Pro Choice

15. INTELLECTUAL PROPERTY

Living on welfare as a single mother in Scotland, J.K. Rowling would push the stroller through the cold city streets then rush into a cafe to write, until her daughter woke up. After seven years of struggling to write the first Harry Potter book, she was turned down by nearly every publisher in the U.K. When her book was finally picked up for publication by Bloomsbury Books, the editor told her she should keep her day job. However, her books went on to be a huge success.

The Harry Potter series of books have sold in the range of 450 million copies and are now considered the best-selling book series in history. J.K. Rowling has a net worth in the range of 500 million dollars. This is the power of intellectual property. It is easier now than ever before to harness this power.

Open Playing Field

Internet distribution channels such as Amazon and iTunes have leveled the playing field where it is possible now for anyone to have their creative works offered to the masses. If you have creative tendencies in music, art or writing, you are now able to create an additional stream of income. Even if you do not have these skills yourself, you may know someone you could partner with to release and market some new products.

> As intellectual property can be speculative I would not recommend investing more than 5% or 10% of your total investment funds in this area.

Investing in intellectual property should be done with funds you can afford to risk, but the payoff, if successful, can far outweigh the risks.

The most important factor to weigh in when pricing out the return on intellectual property channels is the cost of marketing. For making any sort of a profit in these areas clever marketing is key. This also can be a good time to hone your marketing skills and get some hands on practice.

Your creations may not be as magical as Harry Potter, but they can be good places to put your dollars to work, earning more dollars.

Pro Choice

16. ALTERNATIVE INVESTMENTS

Originally hailing from Brazil, Leda Braga dispels all female stereotypes, from riding a Ducati motorcycle to running one of the largest hedge funds in the world with ice cold scientific-based decision making. Her fund, Systematica, uses a "managed futures" strategy, meaning it trades the futures contracts of stocks, bonds, currencies and commodities looking for trends in the movements of their prices. This strategy gained an average of 11.2 percent net of fees, each year from 2004 through 2014, according to performance figures obtained by CNBC.com and has only lost money in a single year, 2013.

Limitless Opportunities

There are as many investment opportunities as the mind can imagine. These alternative investments range from rather conservative limited partnerships, to the wild casino ride of currency trading.

Municipal Bonds

Tax-free municipal bonds can be one of the most conservative investments, yet is one investment that should be considered and understood as wealth increases. These are bonds issued by localities to finance the building of infrastructure such as roads and bridges. Tax-free "munis" are the cornerstone of the investment portfolio of many wealthy people I know. The fact that they do not raise adjusted gross income is a big benefit to those with high incomes who risk getting catapulted into higher tax brackets.

It is important to note that these investments are relatively safe, but not risk-free. Entire cities have been known to go bankrupt, defaulting on all their bond obligations. Bonds also have risk when interest rates increase, this can lower the principle balance as the yield must be adjusted upward to match new demand. Still, the tax-free aspect and higher yields of these bonds make these risks tolerable. Having the local advantage of knowing the projects you are investing in can also serve you well.

Publicly Traded Partnerships

Many limited partnerships are available as publicly traded investment opportunities. These are rather conservative investments, generally used to finance expansion of oil and gas pipelines. With the falling oil prices right now these are not the best investments to be in at the moment, but are still worth considering buying when the prices drop, assuming the companies have strong financials.

Limited partnerships can have big tax benefits as they are structured to create passive losses even while they have distributions they pay out. These passive losses can offset other income, lowering overall tax liability. However, this can come back to bite you when you sell them as these losses lower your tax basis, meaning you can owe taxes when selling, even when selling at a net loss.

Hedge Funds

In general, hedge funds have not paid off. Historically, only 5% of hedge funds beat the S&P 500 index. With much higher fees than index funds carry, these are a poor investment in most cases.

In 1993 hedge funds beat the index on average by 20 percentage points, rocketing them into the realm of super stardom, but they have yet to repeat those glamorous returns.

In 1998 hedge funds as a whole also outperformed the S&P by returning a loss of 19% average compared with 37% average loss of the index.

The one bright light in the hedge fund world is that woman owned and run funds that have outperformed their male counterparts recently.

> In 2012, a sample group of 67 female hedge fund managers had an average return of 8.95%, compared to their male counterparts with a paltry return of only 2.69%.

Leda Braga is leading this new crowd of female hedge fund managers, giving women in the financial world new encouragement. Her background was not originally in finance; she received a PhD in engineering and worked as a researcher and professor before switching to the financial world. She has brought her calculated scientific method to hedge funds and is showing what can be done in this world unfettered by standard investment limitations.

Currency Trading

You may be just as well off gambling your money in the casino as taking part in currency trading. Remember, if something sounds too good to be true, it probably is. I've known some people who have made a lot of money by trading currency, but they also are the same people who have profited off football and poker.

Not to say that this can't be profitable at

times. But owning currency is owning money, not anything of underlying value. Therefore, in the long run, it will not be an investment as much as a store of value.

Precious Metals

Buying gold and silver is much the same as currency trading. It can have huge upswings at times and can be a safe store of money in between investments. There was a time when I could not find any stocks I wanted to buy as they all seemed overpriced and I bought gold instead. This proved a wise decision as the stock market dropped and gold went up. But eventually, as the stock market recovered, holding on to that gold wasn't worthwhile.

There are times when it is hard to find anything that seems like a bargain. At those times it is best to own cash and gold is the most ancient store of value there is.

Pro Choice

Pro Choice

174

17. AGE-BASED INVESTING

If you are 25 or 50 your investment choices and what to do will vary greatly. In each stage of your life it is important that you craft your investment picture to fit who you are and where you are at. This is a quick guide to which investments may be best depending on your decade, although this will need to be adapted to fit you individual life, goals and situation.

In Your Twenties...

When you are young your money has the greatest amount of time to grow from the magic of compounding interest. The other side of the coin is saving for retirement often is a low priority compared with fun and adventures, or just earning enough to get by.

This is the time to get to know yourself. Trade stocks actively to gain financial skills. What you learn now will help you for life.

Opening a Roth IRA with an online broker is one of the best investments you can make now. Time is on your side, so the benefits of the Roth IRA will outweigh the downside of not having an immediate tax deduction over time. Also, you can always withdraw the principal you contributed to a Roth IRA without penalties, meaning you can use this as an "emergency" account to work on getting at least six months' worth of wages set aside.

Yes, it takes time to build a safety net, but the freedom it gives you is well worth it. You never know when your company will be bought out or a natural disaster hits. It is good to have something set aside for the unexpected.

Contrary to what most people think, I don't believe when you are in your 20's is the best time to quit your job and start a business. I did plenty of that and had many setbacks and expensive mistakes. It is far easier to learn the skills you will need working for someone else, then branch out on your own when you are ready. Sometimes this is not possible and due to economy or circumstance you must create your own job. That is fine, but be ready to work harder than you ever imagined to make your business a success.

Thirties....

When you have entered your thirties priorities often shift a bit. Family and career demands can easily take up the time and resources that would otherwise go to investing. It is imperative at this time in your life to have a solid plan you are following and move forward, step by step, fulfilling this.

Roth IRAs can still be a good choice for investment until you earn more than the contribution limit income levels. Maxing out the contribution amounts is critical in this phase as this is the prime time to set aside funds where they will still have time to aggressively grow.

Real estate can also be a good investment now. You probably have enough credit and experience with houses to buy something good as a rental or vacation home and make a profit. Plus the timeline until retirement gives the property time to appreciate and gain value.

This is likely the best time in your life to start a business. You have learned enough career skills and are tempered enough to not make many foolish mistakes, yet you are still young enough to bounce back from failure and become successful.

Forties...

Women in their forties often start to feel the pressures of retirement savings. This is when you need to start making hard decisions about how much money you will need in retirement and what your realistic goals are for the future.

IRAs can be good investments. A Roth IRA is the best choice if you are in the income level where that is still good. Although this starts to be the time when a traditional IRA and current tax savings may be more beneficial than the Roth IRA.

This can also be a great time to think for the future and buy that home you may want to retire in someday. With a 15 or 20 year loan it will be paid off by the time you want to retire and in the meanwhile the renters will be paying most of the costs.

If you have not already done so, this is an ideal time in your life to start a business, perhaps a side line consulting or a hobby business to explore a career path you've always dreamed of trying. You are in a unique position to make your dreams come true. Just remember, it is best to have your first business be in an area you know well rather than trying to learn a new career while launching a business.

Fifties and Beyond...

By this time you are likely well aware retirement is just around the corner. The focus should start to shift from saving and building up a nest egg, to maintaining the assets you have acquired so they can last through retirement.

Traditional IRA contributions are now usually more beneficial than Roth. Now the tax benefits will likely trump the Roth advantage of tax free distributions.

Alternative investments such as publicly traded partnerships and tax free municipal bonds can be beneficial for minimizing tax exposure while keeping investments active. Also these investments are generally rather safe stores of wealth compared with risky stock market investments. A big loss at this time would not be good.

If you own investment real estate, you may wish to do a 1031 exchange to a different rental property that is located in an area you would want to retire in. It is always good to look are real estate purchases and sales with a long timeline ahead, if the values are up on property you bought in the past then this may be a great time to sell and reinvest the dollars to fit your future plans.

Pro Choice

Pro Choice

Appendix

Amoruso, S. (2014). *#Girlboss* [Kindle Version]. Retrieved from Amazon.com

Carter, N. M., & Wagner, H. M., (2011, March 1). *The Bottom Line: Corporate Performance and Women's Representation on Boards (2004-2008).* Retrieved from http://www.catalyst.org/knowledge/bottom-line-corporate-performance-and-womens-representation-boards-20042008

Cash Quotes. (2014, December 13). Patsy Cline. Retrieved from http://www.brainyquote.com/quotes/key words/cash_3.html

Catalyst, (2014, December 11). *Women CEOs of the S&P 500*. Retrieved from http://www.catalyst.org/knowledge/wome n-ceos-fortune-1000

Corcoran, B. (2003). *Shark Tales: How I turned $1000 into a Billion Dollar Business* [Kindle Version]. Retrieved from Amazon.com

Geraldine Weiss: High Quality out of Favour Blue Chip Stocks. (2010). Retrieved from http://www.valuepickr.com/resources/gur u-stock-screens/geraldine-weiss-stock-scre ener-strategy

Jones, M. , Asaro, C., Easterling, K., Farrington, D., Haugerud, R., Jacobsen, C., Kalliaras, A., Mandel, R., Newby, S., Padnos, C., & Pries, S. (2012, December). *Women in Alternative Investments: Building Momentum in 2013 and Beyond*. Retrieved from https://nyhfr.org/documents/FG/hfrt/edu /70046_RK_WomeninAlternativeInvestm entsF.pdf

Michie, J., Aesop, & Lord, J. V. (1989). *Aesop's Fables*. London: Cape.

Nemy, E. (2013, August 25). Muriel Siebert, a Determined Trailblazer for Women on Wall Street, Dies at 84. *The New York Times*. Retrieved from http://www.nytimes.com/2013/08/26/business/muriel-siebert-first-woman-to-own-a-seat-on-wall-st-dies-at-80.html?pagewanted=all&_r=0

O'Connor, C. (2012, April 2). Top Five Startup Tips from Spanx Billionaire Sara Blakely. Retrieved from http://finance.yahoo.com/news/top-five-startup-tips-spanx-161744263.html

Rappaport, A., Butria, B., Hounsell, C., Levering, C., Lump, J., & Siegel, S. (2012, November). *The Impact of Running out of Money in Retirement*. Retrieved from https://www.soa.org/Research/Research-Projects/Pension/Running-Out-of-Money.aspx

Siebert, M. & Ball, A. L. (2002). *Changing the Rules: Adventures of a Wall Street Maverick*. New York: The Free Press.

United States Census Bureau. (2014). Retrieved from http://quickfacts.census.gov/qfd/states/0 0000.html

U. M. Burns. *Lean In*. Retrieved from http://leanin.org/stories/ursula-burns/

Weiss, G., & Lowe, J. (1989). *Dividends Don't Lie: Finding Value in Blue-Chip Stocks*. Dearborn Financial Publishing, Inc.

Pro Choice

Pro Choice

INDEX

pharmaceutical, 117

pipelines, 169

portfolio, 13, 36-37, 46, 97, 121, 168

poverty, 11

premier, 111

premium, 108

preparation, 21, 76

princess, 5-6

principle, 169

publication, 163

publicly, 169, 180

publisher, 163

ramen, 33

ratio, 143

reform, 70

refund, 72, 78, 96

refundable, 78

reimbursement, 75

reinvest, 24, 27, 99, 180

wallet, 35, 42

wardrobe, 52, 63-64, 66

warrant, 24, 101

warrants, 142

wealth, 6-7, 15-16, 28, 31, 50, 81, 168, 180

wealthy, 44, 148, 168

Weiss, Geraldine, 137-142

welfare, 163

Winfrey, Oprah, 11, 15

workday, 34-35

worker, 134

workers, 25, 44

yield, 140, 169

yields, 36, 66, 138, 140, 169

Pro Choice

Pro Choice

ABOUT THE AUTHOR

Crystal Stranger, President of 1st Tax Inc., and author of *The Small Business Tax Guide* (Clear Advantage, 2014), is not your average accountant. As a teen, Crystal read every book in the library on investment while living in a 17' trailer, officially homeless, and working three jobs. Within a year she saved a down payment, buying her first house at age 21. She was a millionaire by 26, owning several businesses and a large real estate portfolio. Using many creative investment strategies, no accountant could say clearly how much tax would be owed. Curious about taxes, Crystal pursued a tax educational program, becoming an Enrolled Agent, and an expert on small business tax law. Through 1stTax.com, she helps start-ups save money on tax and build efficient operations, and writes books to share her knowledge on financial and investment topics with budding entrepreneurs and investors.

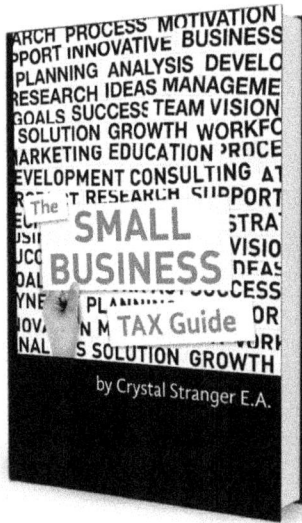

The Small Business Tax Guide: Take Advantage of Often Missed Deductions and Credits to Keep Your Money Where It Belongs- Working For Your Business!
by Crystal Stranger, EA

Tax laws can be your best friend or your worst enemy, it is all how you plan your business activities. Crystal Stranger EA shares her wealth of tax knowledge in The Small Business Tax Guide, presenting numerous money saving techniques to have more capital to reinvest in your business each year. Regardless of if you have a start-up or multi-national firm you will learn how to:

Find valuable deductions and credits that will save you big money legally based on amounts you already spend.

Plan future expenditures around tax savings to maximize the capital available for growth.

Tips to avoid common pitfalls and unscrupulous tax advisors who will cost you far more than any tax savings they advertise.

Ready to save big money on your taxes each year? Read The Small Business Tax Guide and discover how to make tax laws work in your benefit.

www.ingramcontent.com/pod-product-compliance
Lightning Source LLC
Chambersburg PA
CBHW070310200326
41518CB00010B/1956